No One Would Listen

No One Would Listen

Dawn Renna

To order additional copies of this book, contact:
Xlibris Corporation
1-888-795-4274
www.Xlibris.com
Orders@Xlibris.com
53769

This book is dedicated to my mother Connie Deluca who raised me as her own daughter I miss you and love you.

I also like to dedicate this book to my children Angelo, Toniann, Michael and Kenny and also my granddaughter Marianna whom I love dearly I could not have come this far if it was not for you all. You are my inspiration, my love to all of you remember all things are possible as long as you have faith and believe in god and most of all believe in yourself dreams do come true. A pastor once told me miracles just don't happen but you make them happen once you release you faith in god.

I would also like to thank sister Brenda who stood by me when everyone else turned away. You are my spiritual sister for now and forever more I love you. You were there in the beginning and you'll be there in the end. You will always be my closest and dearest friend

With all my love,
Dawn

CHAPTER 1

MY NAME IS Dawn Renna and I am a survivor victim of domestic violence. I am writing this book because I know my story will help other victims like me move on with their life.

I am a 40 yr old mother of four, and grandmother of little girl. I grew up in Brooklyn N.Y on Manhattan Ave. Since the time I could remember my life was nothing but being around abuse.

My parents were alcoholics, my mother worked for W.R. Grace Incorporation and my father was a mechanic. We lived in a railroad apartment two bedroom one bath.

I had an older brother whom my mother had from a previous marriage, my father abused him all the time. My dad didn't like him because he was another man's son; my dad was a very jealous man. My mother was not allowed out of the house only to go to work but she had to come straight home and if she were late he would hit her. My dad was also a bigamist married to another woman and he had seven kids before me. He never abused his other wife or his other kids. My mother supported him and he in turn supported his other wife.

My brother was 12 yrs old when I came along and he had to take care of me and clean the house.

I heard that one day when my brother cleaned the kitchen. He didn't through oil away that was on the stove so my dad beat him. My brother spent a lot of time at my aunt house whom lived in Oakland, New Jersey back then.

When I was two months old, my parents were walking in the snow under the Brooklyn Queen's expressway looking for someone to watch me. They told me that it was because she had to work but the truth was his first wife wanted me dead so I was told they were looking for a place to hide me. But whatever the reason that was the day a 14yr-old girl found me and brought me home to her parents and asked if they could watch me for that woman name was Connie Deluca whom then became my mother.

Her husband Joe made her quite her job to take care of me and they opened their heart and home to me, and called me her daughter. Now I had a sister and two more brothers.

My biological mother had become very close friends with the Deluca's. One day when my brother took me over to Connie house, it was freezing outside and my mother didn't change me and sent me there I was full of piss from head to toe. Connie husband said that was it, I was not going to go home with my parents I was to stay with them.

They put me in between both of them to get me warm they said I was so small they put me in draw to sleep the crib was too big for me. They told me a story about when my mother and father were going to a wedding and when my father seen my mother all dressed up he wanted to have sex but my mom didn't want to so he threw her on the bed and raped her only back in those day's it was not considered rape.

My mother was scared of my dad he controlled her every move. I didn't understand any of it. The only thing I knew was I was the child that was not meant to be. From the time I could remember I always wished I was born into different family all I ever wanted was to be loved.

Well growing up with Connie there was a lot of stuff I had learned about. When I was four years old her husband died. He had loved me so much, I remember one day he had came home from work with a pair of clogs. They were so pretty they had flowers all over the front of them he had brought them for me, except they were to big so he ran back to the store and exchanged them. The second pair was too small he made about four or five trips before he got what he wanted for me.

I remember when I was four years old, I was standing at the top of the banister which was of black iron in only a t-shirt and panties. Everyone ran down the stairs screaming and left me up there. I was scared but didn't understand what was happening. Well the lady across the street from us ran up put a towel around me and took me to her home.

The reason was that my daddy Joe went to work that morning and took a massive heart attack. On the way to work, he walked to work in the morning he worked for Goodman brothers.

That was the last time every seen my daddy Joe.

I always said if he didn't die my life would have been different. I was told that they were going to adopt me but when he died, mom Connie didn't want me to grow up with out a father which now I know I would have been better off,

When I was fourteen years old my father was down stairs sitting outside with his friends drinking. He followed me upstairs and pushed me down on the bed. He was drunk when he drank beer he wasn't that bad but when he drank brandy it was bad.

I had made a police report and it was going through the court system until they told me I was killing my mother and I should drop all charges. So I did I thought I was the cause of it all.

It took me a really long time to realize it was not my fault I grew up very fast.

I loved Connie with everything I had. She had two sons that were battling drug addiction. At that time I saw one instinct were she had tied Joe to the bed in restraints to try and help him. It was a struggle for him and Charlie but they over came there obstacles and have beautiful kids and became drug free and lived productive lives. They loved me dearly. They were my brothers.

But even with all I seen that her sons went through with drugs, you would think I would not have touch drugs. The devil had a hold on me when I was fourteen. I met my son Angelo's dad. He was working in a store on Grand street. He was twenty years old, I fell in love with him. I was always attracted to older men. I now know it was because I was looking for fatherly love.

If you would have told me that then I would have said you were crazy but any way he had turned me on to cocaine sniffing it. At the time also to mescaline I used only on weekends and then everyday.

See the other thing with me was I was only attracted to men who would yell or hit me. But see Angel never did anything like. That he yelled. But by the time I was twenty years old I thought I was missing something and left him.

I had AJ who was three years old then. I was now always using cocaine but not every one knew it my father was still controlling me. I use to love to right so I wrote this poem that a counselor had read and they decided I need help. I had now become suicidal and was put into a psych unit. They said I was bipolar, I didn't understand it back then but come to find out it was not bipolar.

I met this man and we dated for a while. I then became pregnant to my daughter by this time I was using more than ever. I used the drugs so I wouldn't feel anything because now all I was dating was abusive men that were old and controlling. But I had no one to turn to. No one would listen everything was always my fault. I could not please any one no matter how hard I tried.

I always wished I was someone else. I use to yell at God and ask why am I here, please take me. I didn't want to feel anymore but I thought suicide was the answer. But evidently God didn't even want me that was what I thought.

See I wasn't a pretty girl. I had no friends unless I was treating them to something. I always bought my friends because all I ever wanted was to fit in or be loved. I really never had love the way they said I love you in my house was f – you.

But it was ok because I knew Connie loved me. If it was not for her I would have been dead, I know that.

My daughter was born on March.24, 1989. When she was born, she was always sick every two months. Same date she would wind up in the hospital with ammonia.

I had met a man named Thomas whom was in jail at the time but see he told me everything I wanted to hear. So my mother-in law had told me about this hospital, Columbia Prespertieria All Children Hospital. Well I took her there and after twelve months of being in the hospital every two months, she finally was diagnosed with Shwackmen Diamond Syndrome. It comes from Africa there are only nine cases in the whole United States. She was number nine.

Well I lived in the hospital with her for three months straight, never left her side but they had taught me how to put an N.G tube down her nose so she would thrive. She had pancreases insufficiency and need the tube to help her gain weight. She was not supposed to live past a year old, but she did. Well through all this I had met a man named Blass whom I left my husband for. I was with Blass for a year and then became pregnant with Michael. Well Blass used to beat me real bad to were I was black and blue all over. I lost my daughter to the system they screw me over.

There was a lot of money involved when it came to her being disabled and stuff but because of my situation with Blass, I used more drugs than ever.

We would be sitting watching TV and out of the blue, he would hall off and starts punching me. Once again every one blamed me. I even thought it was me. I would say well maybe if I would have done this different or maybe if I didn't nag him so much or make him mad he wouldn't have hit me.

There was one night he wanted sex and I had just had Michael and I couldn't have sex for six weeks cause I had c-section. He took the baby out of my arms and threw me on the bed ripped my night gown off and started having sex with me. Ripped my stitches and told me to shut up and started to hit me.

I was too scared to say anything to any one he worked for the criminal court system in Queens so he had a lot of friends.

CHAPTER 2

THE MORE HE hit me the more I used, I didn't want to feel anything. But now when I look back it was just history repeating itself. Everything I grew up seeing as a child was now happening to me. Its just a viscous cycle that just continue and keeps on going through your family.

Blass had two ex wife and was an ex boxer. He was professional boxer in Puerto Rico. His mother was in nursing home with Alzheimer. He started cheating on me with his ex wife Nancy. She thought she was all that. They had a seventeen year old son. And Blass started sneaking her into my home right after Michael was born but everyone said oh your crazy. The more he cheated the more I would get hit, the more scared I got, the more he raped me.

One day, we went out to a restaurant with my biological mother. Michael was fifteen months old and was not doing anything wrong. Blass picked him up by his neck and threw him in the booth. I knew then I had to do something to protect my child but what would I do I couldn't turn to any one not law enforcement not family. No one would listen, how do I protect my child when I can't protect myself.

So I lied to Blass and said I wanted to go visit a very close friend of mine whom lived in Florida. At this time, I was going to N.A meeting and had a Sponsor. She wasn't happy with my decision, she said I was running away from my problem which was admitting I had a drug problem. She had no clue yes I was running but it was for safety for me and my child. I didn't expect her to understand for no one else did.

So anyway Blass said I could go but had to be back in two weeks. I agreed and said well only make reservation for one way because I have to make sure I can get a ride back to the airport on a certain day. So that was what he did. He knew I was petrified of him and would not betray him so he thought.

I arrived in Tampa on January 6, 1996. I was scared because I really didn't know anyone here.

Michael was two years old and I had never been on a plane before so you can imagine how scared I was. Michael in the middle of the flight said mommy we go home now, he thought we were just going for a ride ha-ha.

We landed at midnight and I had no clue as to what was my next step. I took a taxi to Clearwater a super 8 motel. I only had $200.00 dollars in my pocket, no friends and nowhere to turn to. I called my family, mom Connie and she was so upset that I left but they all said I would be back. They didn't believe I wasn't coming back.

Now I was in this state where no one knew me or where I came from, I had nowhere to live, no job, just my little boy.

What was I going to do I thought to myself, maybe I should have stayed there but he would have killed us. I knew I had to find a cheaper motel in Florida. They have these places you can live for a week for $165.00 a week. That was a lot for me, after all I had no job. I spent 2 days in the Super 8 in Clearwater and then met someone who told me about El P0atio Motel, I went there.

The owners were Indian, very lovely people. I told them my situation and I called my mother and told her I was in what they called an efficiency apartment. It was cute had two beds kitchenette and bathroom. My mom started paying the room with her credit card. I didn't tell her I had no food but the only thing I had was ketchup and milk and coffee. Michael ate ketchup for two weeks until my SSI check came. I had to try and find a job but had no skills the only skills I had were using drugs and know I was drug free cause I knew no one.

I spoke to my family a lot. I was so scared and alone but I didn't want to go back. I lived in Brooklyn all of my life and knew nothing else.

I remember Connie saying to me over the phone how you could leave me. No one understood what I was really going through hell even with me trying suicide 11 times. Even god didn't want me that was what I said.

I prayed at night for him to take me and to spare my life and I hated myself. My mother knew I was struggling and she decided to send me he credit card.

I went to bob evens for a job and worked there for two weeks. The owner of the motel watched Mike for me. They would bring us food and coffee. When I received my mother's credit card, I asked her if I could get an apartment. I would take a cash advance off her credit card, she said yes. I believe it was cause she felt guilty for not being a real mother too me. See now my dad was dead and its funny the day he died she gave up drinking. That showed me that it was cause of him she drank.

I had gotten a cute apartment on a complex called Mallard Point Apartment. Two bedroom, two baths. I took this girl in as a room mate. Trisha that was a mistake, she was into drugs. I threw her out but she had two friends John and Jessie.

I started dating Jessie, not very good thing to do when you just get out of bad relationship. But I was lonely, oh I thought he was great.

After two months I had gotten a great job and everything seem to be going really good. Blass kept calling my mother asking when is she coming back, he was pissed.

My mother told him I was not coming back. Well he wound up in nursing home with Alzheimer. The doctors said he was punched drunk from being a boxer. Go figure, God paid him back for what he did to me.

But any way the man I was dating and his friend moved in with me. he never loved me or actually felt anything for me. He was controlling once my money was gone surprise so was he.

I didn't like the way he treated Michael. Yes at first all they did was play and then he would hit him with a belt if he didn't listen. Michael was not use to sleeping alone, he always slept with me and always had a TV on. Now Jessie did not like that, so he put him in a room and made him scream him self to sleep. I didn't like him reprimanding my son especially since I just got out of bad relationship.

I know what most of you must be thinking oh my gosh what a slut. But I was just looking to be loved and feel wanted. I didn't know anything else and I always thought oh this one will be different.

It never was different though. Now here I was in another bad relationship. Once my money ran out so did Jessie. Oh God but now I was pregnant again.

Now here I am in Florida no family everything going down drain again. But see I didn't believe in abortion so he had threaten me how he could make me and my unborn child disappear out of Florida. I had good job at Curlew Care Home Elderly Alzheimer Assisted Living Facility.

He made that threat over the phone, my cousin Joe was down hear with me then working same place as me.

The threat Jessie made was over speakerphone every one heard it, I paid it no mind though.

Like I said earlier it was like a vicious circle that just kept repeating itself over and over all because all I wanted was to be loved and feel special.

I was 6 months pregnant when I met Fred I moved in with him right away he was there thru the rest of my pregnancy. I started therapy and working for Charter Behavioral Center. Fred was in his fifty's and me in my thirty's. I started therapy with Marion Citrus Mental Health cause my job said I need some one to talk to. Well what they did was bring up all my childhood emotions especially between me and my dad. They said I had to forgive my parents. How can I forgive my parents when my mother said it was my fault I entice my father. How does a fourteen year old do that to her dad. But see my dad never looked at me like a daughter. He said I wasn't going to amount to anything but a bimbo on a street corner.

You tell me how does a person forgive her parents for that so I had an out burst with the therapist. I told her live my life and then talk to me about forgiveness. After that session they put me on 8 medications at one time Lithium, 1500mgr Zyprexer, Prozac Clonzapain Trazadone theorizing Zoloft and there was one more I can't recall the name. I was a walking zombie and that was no joke.

I am sure you could imagine what I was like but hey I was numb and wasn't feeling anything. But most of all I still didn't feel loved.

CHAPTER 3

ME AND FRED were together five years. We moved on a fifteen acre ranch. I had my dream all my kids except my daughter but I had beautiful home 3 bedroom, 2 bath, fireplace, a horses which were my favorite things. When I was feeling down, I would saddle up the horses and ride and just keep riding. But with all the medication they had me on, I really couldn't function anymore.

If you were talking to me I would look at you but had no clue as to what you were saying or who you even were.

I lived on that ranch for seven years. I was not happy with Fred. Hell now I look back and see I couldn't be happy with anyone. Number one, I wasn't happy with me so I could I be happy with anyone else? I was tired of having to work so hard and pay all bills. I felt Fred didn't want to work cause he knew I would so that made me angry. I started going to Webster College for medical assistant. While I was there I met a girl, we became good friends. Me and my kids spent weekends at her house with her and her husband. He worked for Cemex Block Plant in Ocala, Florida.

Well her and her husband seen I wasn't happy and always complain of Fred and how unhappy I was. Well they said they had this nice man they wanted me to meet. I said no cause I was having some weight issue because of all medication. I was on they said how this man's wife left him and mistreated him. So I said well ok you cook a dinner and I will come.

So they did. This man pulled up in a Suzuki four door little car. Here gets out, this man 6ft 4 289lbs and ugly. I looked at AJ and said son this is not going to happen. He looked at me and laughed and said I know mom.

Well me and Tracy went to the store and when we got back we seen that Harry's car was gone. I said thank god he left he kind of looked like Lurch from the Adams family ha-ha.

Well we walked in and to my surprise, my older son AJ was not there. It turned out Harry took him out so he could drive his car, I was surprised. I mean here this man don't know me or my kids. My son didn't even have a license.

What was this man up to? Well we all ate dinner, Harry stayed for a little while and then said he had to go help his father in law and we all said bye.

The next day Tracy called me and said Harry wanted to take me out to dinner I said no at first. I put him off for close to a week and then I said ok maybe he would leave me alone.

It was Kenny's birthday that next week and Harry had heard us talking about it. He also knew we had no money to give Kenny any thing for his birthday. Well he threw us all in the car and took us to Wal-Mart shopping for Kenny. Wow I was impressed no one ever done that before.

He kept telling how his wife stole from him and ripped off bunk beds. And how she cheated on him while he was at work all the time and he came home from work one day, all her stuff was gone and her kids stuff whom Harry had raised. He also said she was an alcoholic. He laid it on thick, I felt bad for him. All I kept thinking was oh my god this poor man that is so sweet has been hurt so bad.

I have never met a man that had been abused by a woman. My heart went out to him. He said how he gave her everything. And didn't I want to be with someone whom would love me with all there heart and never hurt me. Wow! It sounded like my fairy tail he was going to be my knight and shinning armor. He was going to rescue me from all the bad in my life. I would never hurt again.

On Feb,14 2002 Valentine's Day, I went to visit his daughter at his house. On his table were two dozen red roses and a big chocolate kiss with a beautiful card saying, "I love you. Happy V day."

Well I melted. No one ever did that for me, he was this man whom had great job at Cemex Block Plant, new car and was a perfect man. That was looking for the same things I was which was just to be loved. By real women I fell head over heels.

When I was a little girl I had a dream of being rescued by a prince on a white horse. I thought for sure my prince had arrived.

When we first met the first month we were together, he had to go to west Virginia but I had to work. He begged me to go with him, I couldn't. I worked for a nursing home in Gainesville so he went. Oh he bragged to all his friends and family about me. Said how much of a real woman I was most of all he just kept bragging how much he loved me. He called me around the clock, all his family was amazed how happy he was. They all hated Sara that was his ex wife.

She was not allowed anywhere around his families homes. Anyway when he got back from West Virginia, he said how they can't wait to meet me and they were so happy for him and they just wanted me up there.

Well a month later we went and I met his whole family including his son Chris. He took me to his brother Ronnie house, I met his sister-in-law Suzie which later I found out that was Harry's first wife's sister. Also the day I met her she took me outside and said honey for your sake I hope he's changed and she started telling me the story of how he beat her sister all the time and cheated on her. All I kept thinking was wow, Harry said this woman was crazy cause the stuff she was telling me sounded off the wall.

She told me Harry use to shit in the bowl and rub her face in it and then she said when she was in the shower Harry would piss on her. All I kept thinking was this woman is crazy.

His first wife now lives in a hospital she is schizophrenic and supposable hears voices. She lives on medication and is doing well but when Suzie said it was all Harry's fault, I didn't believe her I thought I knew him better them any one and he was just so sweet and soft spoken.

If you got him mad, he had a temper but you didn't see it often he had this soothing voice that was unbelievable. When people would call me they would say is that really his voice it was one you would only hear on television. He was my hero.

On July 4 2003 I was so excited that day I was picking up my daughter from the airport. It was the first time she was coming for a visit in such a long time. I was walking on a cloud.

Harry let me take his car to the airport to pick her up. My son AJ and his girlfriend at the time followed behind me. On the way home, his ex-girl friend ran me into a semi truck and messed up Harry's car. I broke my foot everyone else was fine, thank God. That was the first time I believe I saw Harry's anger it wasn't toward me it was pointed at my sons girl friend.

He hated her after that I gave him 3000 out of my settlement for a vehicle. Everything after that was ok for a while until Sara his ex wife heard about the accident. See the car that got total was in her name so when she heard about the car and she saw dollar bill signs, she called him every day at work and said she loved him and wanted him back. Well he wanted his cake and eat it to.

The only thing was she was with this other guy in West Virginia she also had her daughter with her whom Harry love and always said that little girl should have been his.

He would choose Sara's kids over his own any day of the week. Once she started calling him at work, Harry started to change he said if I loved him I would leave the ranch were I was living for the past seven years other wise I would lose him forever.

Well I did. I got a really great house three bedroom, two bath in Ocala Park Estate. The first thing he did was call up to West Virginia and told everyone he bought a house. The only thing was it was not his. It was mine and my son AJ and of course my other two little boys.

Well when Sara heard about the house, she defiantly wanted him back at all cost. See Harry wasn't use to living the way I was. He was basically always in trailers, never had nice stuff.

Then here I am nice house furnisher. I had taste and these people didn't, trailer trash that they were.

All of a sudden her brother started hanging around our home and everyone else from her father's trailer park. Little did I know they were setting me up?

Harry always said he could mess with some one's mind and make them think they were going crazy but I always thought he was talking just to hear him self talk but he was not. Right after we moved in it, turns out Sara's boyfriend was molesting her daughter. She knew about it and did nothing. Stood by and let this man do this to her daughter. Harry flipped out, he wanted to kill both of them but he loved her too much to do anything to her. But he also didn't want to leave me either at this point.

See she only wanted him if I was in the picture because she really didn't love him, just his money.

I did everything for this man I cooked for him he use to get home at 4.30 am. I would get up and make sure he had a hot meal when he got in, I would have to meet him at the door, take off his shoes and message his feet. Basically do everything for him like I was his slave. I didn't mind I loved him so much.

I thought if you loved someone, it was ok to do all those things.

But he was laughing at me the whole time. See I was the good one that he would bring to his family and friends. She was the trashy one whom full filled his sexual fantasies.

It was that she was prettier than me cause when she smiled she had teeth like a horse. Harry always said he liked his women trashy and I wasn't trashy enough for him.

It started in my home where I would hear some one call my name or heard noises around the house. Or put something down and it would turn up somewhere else.

Most of the time it would be about five am, I would start hearing all this stuff woman's voice or Harry talking to someone. I had a counselor making home visits. At the time she was from Marion Citrus Mental Health. One night I am laying next to him in the bed and I hear him say I didn't think I loved you anymore but I still do. Then I heard this woman's voice, I couldn't make out what she said but I jumped up and when I went to get out of the bed. Harry threw his whole body on top of me and had me pined down to were I couldn't move. And all of a sudden started to have sex with me he would not let me up and it was very hard to push him off because of how big he was.

While he was forcing sex on me I heard my bedroom door slam but by the time he let me up, it was too late, she was gone.

I couldn't prove she was there. When I ran to my sons room and told him and his girlfriend, they said I was crazy and they continued to smoke their weed.

This went on for a while till I had one of his friends go up into the attic and see if there was anything up there. To our surprise there was a blanket and empty soda cans.

See I couldn't figure out how they knew my every move but they did. He had people following me all over. They would park outside my job. They worked in shifts. The wife of his coworker whom was his supervisor, his wife would follow me. One night these two girls in a blue ford Taurus tried to run me off the road into Dunkin' Donuts window. I had my little boy in the car with me, I called the police and they said stalking is hard to prove. This went on for a while.

Finally when my counselor and her supervisor came over to the house we were all in the kitchen and I said to her would you please tell this fool if I hear voices. He can't answer them when they told him it was impossible. He got pissed off and ask were did they get their licenses out of bubble gum machine.

He was just pissed because they were not buying his story that I was stressed out and hearing voices.

He tried to convince everyone I was crazy. He had my kids believing I was. They now know better.

One night AJ, his friends, and I were trying to hide in the woods, but I didn't realize Harry's friends were watching every move we made. They knew what time I went to the bathroom, they were video taping him and Sara trying to drive me out of my mind.

One night I couldn't take it any more, I heard her begging him to leave me and he said to her it's not that easy I love her too. No he just love the fact that I was his maid.

I jumped up and once again he had me pinned down on the bed and started pulling my pants bottoms off and forced himself on me. I told him to stop but he wouldn't. When he was done, I ripped the house apart. I threw closets down on the floor ripped pictures off the wall and started throwing things at him. He said I was crazy and needed to be committed. Well how was it that I knew these people were in my home but couldn't find them. This went on for several months.

I called my sister Theresa and told her what was going on and she bought me a plain ticket. See there was other stuff going on with my kids that I wasn't aware of. Mike was being picked on in school and never told me and so was Kenny but they didn't tell me. They missed like 20 days of school at that time. I was in no shape, I just determined to prove I was not crazy. But every time I tried I failed.

When Harry heard I was going to N.Y, he flipped and went out and bought me an engagement ring it was gorgeous. It was grand mar keys diamond ½ carrots. I screamed when I seen it. After all, he even got down on one knee and ask me to marry in front of my older son and his girlfriend. I got them out of bed so they could see Harry ask AJ for approval to marry me. My son was so happy for me.

Little did I know it was just to pacify me and keep me happy while he still continued his little game?

See it was the excitement of not getting caught and like I said if I was not in the picture she didn't want him.

That night once again I heard people talking by this time me and my son AJ were at each other cause the child really thought I was losing my mind. The next day when I got up, I made myself coffee and then as always went outside to smoke a cigarette. But I left my keys in the house after I put Mike and Kenny on the bus. I went into the house, well AJ's room was down the hall in the opposite direction of my room. As I was walking into the kitchen, AJ's door opened just a little. I thought it was him so I paid no mind to it. This happened three mornings in a row, after the door would open five minuets later, I would hear the garage door open and then close. I just figured, maybe it was AJ. But later that night, I asked AJ what the hell are you doing every morning peeking out your door, he looked at me like I was crazy. He said mom I am not, it's not me. What are you talking about? Then I knew ok it was her.

Anyway, when I forgot my keys in the house I went into get them and could not find them anywhere. We all searched the house left and right, my keys were nowhere to be found. Harry said I was crazy once again, but see I always left my keys in the same spot every time. We searched for three days. We took cushions off the couches and chairs they just weren't there.

So now I start fighting with Harry because I knew he had them. Somehow, some way I just knew he had them.

That night one of my neighbors gave me a voice activated tape recorder and I hide it in the room because my room smelt like white diamond perfume which he had bought me. But I only put it on if I was going out.

But this night my room smelt like a French whore house. Everyone in the house smelt it, but of course Harry said we were all crazy. I went to sleep, I just didn't care anymore. I had already lost so much sleep.

I wasn't sure if I was hallucinating at this point or not, I was losing my mind. So I hide the tape recorder and went to sleep he was off from work that day. And I decided to look for my keys one more time. Danielle helped me and the same couch we look in before and surprise surprise, there were my keys. They mysteriously reappeared.

So another day, we argued. I called up my councilor and asked her to come right over and of course she did. I let her listen to the tape. After she heard it she said Dawn I knew where not hearing voices but after she left he destroyed the cassette player and all the phones in the house.

My sister paid for a plane ticket and I was on that flight but when I started packing my close in the closet, I found women's clothes that were not mine. They were too big to be mine and when I lifted them up, a key fell out it was a key that opened all the locks in my house including my bedroom door. Now I flipped out and went after him. He laughed and said he will make it look like a burglary and my family won't be able to identify my body.

I thought he was joking and I ignored his threats. So I just took Michael and left for N.Y.

CHAPTER 4

KENNY'S DAD TOOK him. It turned out when I was following Harry, trying to catch them following me, Kenny's dad had a private investigator following me and watching every move I made. Then he said he would go to court and have Michael taken away from me and put in foster care. I panicked because my past history with my daughter set in and how I was screwed by the system so I signed the papers for him to have custody now I regret it. But at the time, I was under distress and he and his mother said if I didn't sign them, they would take my child to Columbia and I would never see him again. I got scared so once again I obeyed a man.

Well I was in N.Y for 3 months and then Harry called and begged me to come back. And of course, I did. He said he was going to kill him self, me like the idiot, I am I ran back he said it would be different. He told Sara get out and that it was over between them while I was on the phone, that her spit couldn't shine my shoes. I loved that part because I thought he was finally done with her and got her out of his system.

Joke was on me all the time though.

He brought me back only to move into a sleaze bag motel were he paid $250.00 a week. I didn't care as long as I was with him.

Everything was good for about a week. his daughter Kelly called me and we were on the phone for almost an hour. I love that girl like she is my own daughter. She don't talk to me anymore. Blood is thicker than water. They say she loves her daddy so much and when he gets mad at her he calls her every name in the book, even a whore like my daddy did me.

She was glad to here I was back with him. She cried, I cried. She has a son Calvin. I was the first one he called grandma. We were all sitting in the living room at Shannon house. When I got up and went near the door and he turn around and said grandma were you going, we all just looked at each other. Kelly and Harry almost died me to for that matter, after all Calvin hardly saw me but yet his grandmother lives next door and I was the first one he called grandma. That made my day.

I will always love Kelly, Todd and Calvin with all my heart for as long as I live. Even if they don't ever speak to me again.

Kelly knows if she ever needs anything I would help her if I could. No doubt about that. I haven't spoken to her in a year now but I think about them all the time.

I know Todd got married to Jill cause right after they got married they called my phone and said tell daddy I got married. I don't know why they new I don't talk to him.

I did a lot for those kids in a short time but never minded any minute of it and t hey knew it.

After I was in Florida for about six months Harry and I broke up again I went back to New York my mother Connie was very sick and I had to get to her.

AJ and Michael were there with me. I didn't realize how sick she was until I seen her in that hospital bed. I wrote her a poem while I was in Florida and I remember calling Theresa on the phone and reading it to her. After that, she had everyone in the family call me just so I could read it to them. I tried reading it to my mother but she couldn't hear and she was stubborn and would not put her ear piece in so when I got to new York I tried to read it to her but she was trying to read my lips. I could not read it with out breaking down she past away on Feb.6,2005. That was the most heart breaking time for me.

When she was gone, I was no longer treated like family anymore and that did they think I was not morning for her she was my best friend. I still say she waited for to see me that day I decided to give. Theresa a break and I was going to sit with her up in the hospital all that day and I had even plan to sleep there if they would have let me.

But god had already decided she was going home with him that day she died looking at me and holding my hand.

I will never forget that last look of her eyes looking straight into mine and grabbed my hand and her eyes rolled back and she was gone. I lost everything that day my mom my best friend and the only one in this world that never turned her back on me. I was alone again, this time for good.

Well I had decided to read her the poem I wrote her while we were having her service her coffin. Was in the middle close to the alter, I got up and said mom you couldn't hear me read it while sitting on your bed. I know you will hear it now. Every one that was there at first thought it was going to be something out of a book but it was all about how I came to her and what she done for me. When I was done, there was not a dry eye in the church, here it is:

A Mother's Love

When I was only two months old
You took me in from out of the cold
Theresa found my parents walking in the snow
And took me home to you,

When you woke up that day,
You had no clue
As to what it was you were
About to do.

You took me in your arms
And held me tight
And kept me safe all through
The night.

Everyone else turned there heads
And made out they didn't see
For they all knew I was the child
Who was never suppose
To be.

You opened your heart
And your home to me
And from that day on
I was part of a real family

Any woman can carry a child
And go through hours of labor
And push a child out
But that don't make her a mother
All of a sudden she is full of doubt
And has no clue as to what being
A mother is all about,

A mother holds you tight
When things go bump in the night
A mother tells you everything's
Going to be alright,

Mom I hold you close in my heart
Its killing me that were apart
Gee I always thought I was so smart
Now I don't even know were to start

Now I sit and watch you lay
In the hospital bed
There is so much I
Should have said

I wish I could take your place
Right now
But that god refuses to allow,

You lay there in so much pain never once did you complain
Yet all I do is cry in vein
And yell at god to explain

How could he take my mom from me?
He said the time has come to set you free
For you to go home to heaven above
Were there is no pain only peace and love.

Mom I yell at you to take me too
You say there still so much for me to do,
I don't want to live with out you.

You're my best friend
Someone on whom I could always depend
No matter what it is I do
I knew I could always count on you.

God sent you down from heaven
Above just so I would have
A real mother's love

I end now by telling you
I love you with all my heart
I know we'll be together
One day in heaven above
And thanks to you I'll always
Remember a real mother's love

P.S I am writing this not to thee
With hopes that she'll always remember me.
I love you Mom Connie.

CHAPTER 5

WE BURIED HER and then I get a call from Harry telling me how sorry he is to hear my mother passed away.

In the next breath he tells me he has a really big problem. He is addicted to crack. I flipped out the one who always lectured me about drugs is now using crack.

His kids had me on the phone. Please Dawn help, my daddy well me thinking I could help him because I always hated crack. Well here I go again, back on the plane to rescue him. No I know what your thinking didn't I learn anything the first time. Well he said she started him on it and he needed me so I went to rescue him . . . again.

Once I was there, he put me up in a motel and he came over after work and said to me oh I have a rock do you want some but then so no I am only kidding. The next night, the same thing except he wasn't kidding he really did have a rock which was crack.

Now I always said I would never touch crack. I hated the smell. Then he came out with if you love me you take just one hit do it I swear its not addicting. Me and my stupid self said you know I love you but I don't want to do you. He said then you really don't love me, used the guilt trip now.

So now not only did I come back to Florida to try and rescue him from killing himself or getting addicted to crack, here I was using again, except the addiction was worse than the addiction to sniffing coke. Crack is a physical addiction were coke is mentally addicting.

So now here he goes buying me drugs keeping me high and beating me verbally, abusing me and controlling my every move. He would belittle me everyday, telling me I was a junkie, crack head and every thing else.

All I kept thinking was how do I get off this and leave him. I was so scared. He had made threats that no one believed, they sounded off the wall. I was strung out on crack for two months bad it was 5.00am in the morning and he ran out of money to get his drugs. He wanted me to sleep with the dealer to pay him off; when I refused he beat me to were I couldn't get out of bed for two days.

His cheating got worse. Me and my kids were watching TV and he came out and said how are you going to feel when you find out you are with a stone cold killer? "I said to him fool if you were a stone cold killer you wouldn't tell me. He looked at me with the coldest eyes you ever seen in your life. He said I will burn this trailer down with you and your kids in it and your family wont be able to identify your body and told me I needed to watch a movie called "Next Of Kin" with Patrick Swazi. I asked him what was it about he said so I could see what red neck hillbillies can get away with. I remember saying to him you need to watch "The Soprano's" so you can see what Sicilians can get away with and he just looked at me.

I had went to Marion county sheriff and told them if anything happen to me they were to look for him cause he was going to have me killed.

They advised me to get a restraining order. I went to county jail and filed for one. Me and my son Michael were there going on four hours now. He was tired; we were just waiting on the judge to approve the temporary order.

Since I still had two more hours to wait, I said I was going to bring my son home and I would be back.

I took Michael to the trailer and I told him don't be scared, it was just a game they were playing to scare me. It would be alright right after I left. When I got back to the jailhouse, I decided to call Michael and check on him.

He was crying and said they were banging on the window and tried to open the door. I screamed for the cop that was there and they sent a car to the house for my son. They said they found tire tracks but no one was there by the time they got there. They were just trying to scare Michael. Harry and Sara have no morals. They don't care about their kids, why should they care about mine.

The judge ordered the temporary order, it was good for thirty days till the court date. Well I got my court date and went to court. Not only was I trying to get a restring order against Harry but also Sara.

The only thing was they could not find Sara to serve her with the papers. They questioned him and he said I was crazy she was living in West Virginia. The sheriff office knew better, but they just couldn't find her. They told him if they found out he was lying he was going to jail.

He didn't care he knew he was good and they wouldn't catch him. The day before I had to go to court, he called me and begged me not to go, thru with the restraining order he pleaded with me. Dawn please you don't know how much I love you. Why are you doing this to me. Once again I felt guilty so I didn't show up in court.

I was still determined to prove I was not crazy to people cause I knew they were all talking about me. Oh she is the crazy one, she hears voices. The cops were so tired of hearing from me that I called them one night and the cop said, oh you're the one who hears cell phones ringing from under the trailer. But still there was one cop deputy ransacks he new something was going on.

I had bought these locks for my front door were you need a key to open it even from the inside. Well one day, me and Harry went to the store because he would always try and get me out of the house by 11 am every morning. But see when I changed the locks, I refused to give him a key so now I made his mind game hard for him.

So we went to the store and when we came back, someone had broke out of my house. Yes, you heard me right broke out of my house, not in.

This deputy said if he didn't see if for himself he would have never believed it.

He looked at Harry and said I know you had something to do with this and if it's the last thing I do, I will prove it

And said I know this girl is not crazy. Oh he was pissed because now the cops knew there was something going on, they just couldn't prove it.

I think toward the end they wanted to catch him more than I did.

On November 9, 2005 there was an incident at 5.00am in the morning were my manager and friend from work had to run to my trailer and get me out. Because he said if I came out of the bedroom, he was going to kill me. I thought he was kidding and when I walked out, he grabbed a kitchen knife and I put my arm up in front of my face and he cut near my wrist area. When he seen I was bleeding, he said if I called the cops he would tell them I tried to kill myself. But if you looked at it, you could tell if I was going to try and kill myself I would not have cut it that way. I worked in the medical field for eleven years, I knew how to do it if I wanted to.

But anyway, Harry didn't know I had my friend Diana on the phone and she was already on her way over. She came, got me out and drove me to Clearwater.

I made a police report and the officer that took the report said we will call you when he is released. I was scared to death because he said if he ever got arrested for domestic violence by me, it was all over. I would never see my kids again.

Surprise, surprise the state attorney refused to prosecute. He said there was not enough evidence. I remember sitting in his office and think, wow this man must be an abuser himself. Those were his famous worse I am sorry there is not enough evidence.

So once again, he got away with it. The state attorney never even questioned my witness.

So now what was I to do? I had no money and no were to go. How would I live? I was scared. I had no job, no place to live and nothing to eat. So I had to crawl back to him and apologize and say I know it was all my fault, I would make it up to him just so I would have a place to stay.

Things went on the same as always for the next couple of months.

But now I started to go into self defense mode. I would sleep with knives under my pillow and I really would fall asleep till he left for work. I was drawn out depressed and scared. I had nowhere to turn, no one to talk to. He had isolated me and made everyone think I was crazy.

He would say things like Poor Dawn no one will listen to her and laugh. I would walk with my head down after he would do all this he would say, honey don't you know how special you are come on snap out of this crazy state your in.

On December 24,2005 he took me to West Virginia for Christmas just to get me away from my kids for the holiday. My kids Kenny was with his dad in Alabama, and Michael was with Fred my heart broke cause Mike didn't even have a Christmas tree and no gifts to open. I never even got to talk to him because of Harry but there was nothing I could have done, I didn't have a choice.

I also had a court date coming up for a traffic violation. I was told I had to be in court on January 6, 2007 by Harry, so he didn't bring me back until January 4, 2007. I had just got a job on January 5, 2007 at McDonald's across from the motel. I was feeling good cause he was letting me work finally even though the money had to go to him.

On January 6, 2007 I called the court to see what time I had to be there and the woman said you were supposed to be here on the 3rd. I had a warrant issued and had to spend ten days in county jail. Now I was really scared and ran up the stairs yelling at him, he just laughed.

It turns out he hid my paper from me. So now here I was, I had to go to jail.

I had never been in trouble before. I was petrified, I waited for the cops to come to my job to get me and when the cop got there, he said I am looking for a guy named don I said sir you are looking for me. He felt bad for me because he knew what I had been going through. In the way to the jail he said to me honey I told you, you need to leave him.

I answered I know but I am scared I have no were to go, even working at McDonald's I was only making $6.50 per hr.

My first three days in the county jail, I did nothing but cry and learned how to pray and ask god for help and to forgive me. I said when I got out I would change.

CHAPTER 6

HARRY CAME TO see me on my second day in there, he was crying oh honey I am sorry I feel for you. All I could think of was you waited two days before you visit me and your crying. What about what you done to me.

At this point I hated him, and all I was doing was thinking of ways to kill him. I said that when I got out if he came at me again, it was going to be either me or him and I made a vow it was not going to be me.

I thought of means and ways on how I was going to defend myself. Like I said I now went into survival mode.

I said I am 38 years old, never been in trouble and now I am in jail for failure to appear because of this man. It was time to turn my life over to got and stand on my feet. I didn't know how, I was still very scared. All I knew was I had to make it through these next few days. I didn't eat much all I did was sleep, it made time go by fast.

On my tenth day in jail at nine am they called my name for me to be released I never moved so fast.

Harry was there to pick me up crying oh honey I missed you I looked at him with such hatred it wasn't even funny.

I told him I had a lot of time to think and things will change. He said I had turned cold toward him. Well hello, maybe I was just getting smart or something. I didn't know what it was but I was ready for anything he threw at me. Now I didn't know what to expect that night, I was frightened and didn't want to sleep. He seen me put the knife under were I could reach it. I told him if he came near me I would kill him. I didn't care anymore, he was a little worried. I didn't sleep much neither did he. Well things were calm for a few weeks.

I knew I was changing but I wasn't sure if it was for the good or the bad. I was loosing myself, it was like I didn't know me.

Well on February 9, 2006, Harry was off from work and he said honey I really want to do something nice for you. I want to take you to a movie and out to eat and shopping.

I could not figure out what he was up to, all I kept thinking was maybe he is sorry for everything he's done. Maybe he realized I am the woman for him, maybe he does love me and I am just crazy. All these thoughts running through my head doubting myself. Thinking ok, maybe I should go for therapy. Could it be I am hearing voices, but if so how is he answering them. All these questions but I had no answer.

Well we went to eat at olive garden, and then went to the movie and then Wal-Mart.

All I kept thinking was this is a great day, he had everything so well planned out but also gained my trust.

Now were in Wal-Mart and he picks me out this huge teddy bear, dozen roses, a beautiful card saying how much he loves me and a nice out fit.

We leave the store and I just glance over at him. I smile and thank him and he said Happy Valentine's Day. I looked at him and said wait, since when do you let me see any gift before the holiday was here. He never did that. He was the type of man that liked to surprise you with gifts on holiday. Ok, what was going on here.

I ignored my gut feeling that something was not right and just tried to enjoy the moment.

So we go back to motel room, were laying there and he takes my hand and said take these a puts 10 muscle relaxes in my mouth and makes me swallow them and said just sleep. Its ok, it'll be done soon.

I remember crying myself to sleep. Oh my God, I am never going to see my kids again. I never got to say goodbye. Oh dear Lord help me. Tell them I love them and never meant for any hurt I caused them. I only wanted to be loved.

I guess I feel asleep. I don't remember much after that, except at 4.30am, being waking up by my night shirt being torn off me. He rolled me on my stomach and he started ramming his penis into my Virginia and me yelling for him to stop. He just laughed and said I know you can handle it. I closed my eyes and prayed he would hurry up and finish.

I heard laughing in the room but couldn't see anything. He had my shoulders pinned down to the bed, I could not move.

After he finished he started to cry. I said what's the matter with you and he said I never meant to hurt you, I really do love you

I found myself consoling this man but see at this time I still was not aware it was rape.

I woke up the next morning sore and hurting real bad. He let me stay in bed that whole day with out bothering me.

He went to work about 3:30 PM and that was when I really felt safe enough to go into a deep sleep because I knew he wouldn't be back till 4.00am.

When he got in at 4.00am, I woke up and had to make him something to eat and of course meet him at the door, take his work boots off and rub his feet. He said that was what my job was.

He went into the shower and I laid down not before I put a big butcher knife under the bed mattress were I could get to it easy. See I had planned if he came at me, I was going to stab him to death before he hurt me. This was my self defense mode I went into.

I fell asleep before he got out of the shower, well between 4.30 and 5.00. I was awoke by him ripping my night shirt up I was laying on my right side and he rammed his penis into me from behind. The pain was excruciating, I remember it like it was yesterday.

After a few moments he turned me on my back and continued. I begged him to stop after he first penetrated me, but he ignored me so I yelled again No and please stop.

He told me shut up I have the right to do this I obeyed.

I thought of how can I get to the knife, but I knew I couldn't reach it and then I thought if I do reach it, he is a lot more powerful than me. He will use it on me and I didn't want to die that way.

When he was done I ran to the shower and sat in the tub scrubbing myself. I felt so dirty and disgusted, I couldn't get clean no matter how hard I scrub. But I knew this was the last straw, I had enough. I just was not sure how to leave.

I had to think of a plan or lie or something. Otherwise, I was as good as dead.

On February.11, 2006 at ten o'clock at night, I called information for a domestic violence shelter. Harry was in the shower, it was his day off from work. I called the shelter and to my surprise, it was located very close to were I was.

When I heard him getting out of shower I told the woman on the phone I would get back in touch with her.

At eleven P.M we were watching country music channel and Carrie Underwood came on singing "Jesus take the wheel". It was like something inside me clicked. I looked at him and said, I wanted to go to a N.A meeting that was located up the street he said I had to be back no later than thirty minutes.

I said don't worry, I will be back on time. "he said take the truck". He knew if I had the truck, I was definitely be back. I said I needed to walk and get my thoughts together. He finally agreed.

I ran down the street so fast my heart was racing. I knew he would not be far behind.

I finally found the place and did what they call my intake. After we were done, I said to her I have to go back for some of my stuff. I left with nothing. She was not happy about me going back to get my stuff, she said honey you are not safe please stay. It must have been the look in my eyes. Because I assured her I would be back in a few minutes.

She reached inside her desk draw and said take this cell phone, it was a phone that only dialed 911. I told her give me twenty minuets to get back, I I knew she was scared for me. I seen it in her eyes.

But I wasn't going with out my cloths and stuff. I made it back to the room exactly at midnight. He was furious because I was late, I said to him I was going in a rehab cause I needed help. I had to make up a story so he would let me out without hitting me.

He sat up on the end of the bed and said "if you go I will kill myself" "You don't know how much I love you".

I walked over to him gave him a big hug and said" I love you to and you are about to find out just how much". I will never forget the look on his face.

He insisted on driving me, I said it was not permitted I could not get visits so I had to take a cab. He bought it and paid for my cab.

The councilor was relieved when I walked back through that door. I was scared to death, I had never been in a battered women shelter before and didn't know what to expect.

I was afraid to sleep. I sat up and walked the floors all that night. I was missing him so much and didn't know why.

I went up front to talk to the counselor and asked if it was normal for me to miss him? I didn't understand what I was feeling, "how could I miss this man who was hurting me so bad?

I came close to going back to the motel room but I fought that feeling because I knew if I did it was all over.

That was the night I learned to pray really hard. I asked god to help me.

After I was lying in my bed I started to cry and once again went up to the front desk, she knew I was scared. I had never been in a shelter before and told me if I needed to talk she was available all night.

I finally took her up on her offer; I started asking questions and started to open up to her more about my story.

I told her what happened the night before. How he had sex with me and yelled for him to stop. I will never forget the way she looked at me and said "honey you do know that is rape". I answered no because he was my boyfriend how could it be rape. She asked me "did you say no". Well yes I yelled for him to stop because it was hurting but he just laughed.

She handed me a pamphlet and said I should read it, after I read it all I could do was cry.

Now I felt more disgusting and dirty than I did before. Not to mention ashamed I worked in the medical field for 10 years. I had training on domestic violence and other training sexual abuse, abuse on the elderly. How could I have been so stupid?

She asked if I wanted to call police and make a report, I was just so scared and embarrassed. All I kept thinking is, oh my God he will definitely kill me if I make a report.

I went back to my room and laid there and cry more.

I tossed and turned all night I think I finally fell asleep about 6 AM that morning.

When I woke up there was a different consular at the front desk. I asked her if I could use the phone. I wanted to make a police report.

She took me into an office and let me use the phone to call Ocala City Police Department to file a report. I was shaking the whole time I was on the phone.

A deputy came out and took me in a room were we would have privacy and no one would here our conversation. It was a male officer, I really didn't feel comfortable talking to him but I had no choice. He was the one they sent.

I could not believe his response to me, "I am sorry but I can't label it as rape most couple's like it rough". My mouth dropped I walked out of the office and went over to were the counselor was sitting. She looked at me and I asked the officer to repeat what he had just said to me. He did, I was shocked. How could he have said that, he made me feel like dirt.

My response to him was, "I am not most people". Now I was angry. All I kept thinking was, oh my God Harry was right. No one would listen to me. They would laugh at me.

My hope was gone.

I then asked the officer take me for an exam. I was still very sore and swollen and had fresh burses. I said they could use a rape kit to prove I was raped by this man. Once again his response was" we only use rape kits to find out who's DNA. It is but they don't do rape kits on victims that are in a relationship with the person they said raped them because most people like it rough.

I was so glad he said it in front of this consular.

I just put my head down and said, Harry wins again, and went to my room.

How could the system be like this, who protects the victims, everyone turn their heads especially the law enforcement.

No one wants to listen if its domestic violence so were is a person to turn for protection.

A couple of days later they sent a detective to take my statement but I really didn't want to talk to her, why should I waste my breath, time or effort what was she going to do.

I remember in the last part of my statement. I said to her, "funny I usually had to beg him to touch me he never would. I looked up at her after I said it, and I can hear her voice as if it was yesterday, "You mean to tell me you had to beg this man for sex and now out of the clear blue two nights in a row he got a sex drive? I just looked and put my head down with shame.

If it was up to her I believe deep down in my soul he would have been arrested but now she had to go to state attorney and get a warrant.

I knew the outcome the state attorney favorite response to me was I am sorry honey there just is not enough evidence for me to build a case. Well maybe there would have been if he would have spoke to my witness that one day, but he had refused.

I remember saying to him what do you have to wait till he kills me or beats me half to death before you arrest him. To my disbelief his response was "yes I am sorry" and that was the end of our conversation.

Two weeks went by and I heard nothing from the detective. Finally, on a Monday afternoon, I received the message that they were not going to prosecute because the state attorney said there was not enough evidence. How could there be evidence when the cop wouldn't label it as rape or even take me to the hospital to get checked.

I was discouraged and hurt and angry. I decided that my voice would be heard.

I was not sure who I was contacting or even going to turn to help but I knew my voice would be heard somewhere.

I refused to let this man win. I had to tell someone my story and see if they would listen.

Who would I tell though, was he right was I crazy, was this all my fault.

I started to feel more worthless now than ever but this time I was filled with anger.

I was determined to do something that night I laid in my bunk bed and cried and prayed and ask the Lord to help me. Once again, I turned all my faith on God. I didn't know what my next step was going to be but I knew it was going to be a big step because no I was on a mission.

Several thoughts ran through my head that night. I didn't get much sleep. Where would I start, who would I call, were do I go from here.

I finally fell asleep.

CHAPTER 7

THE NEXT MORNING when I woke up at nine A.M, I went to the front desk and asked them if I could go to the library. They gave me a voucher for the bus.

I had never taken a bus in Ocala before. I had no clue where to get the bus or even what time it ran. One of the other girls came with me, we arrived there about three P.M and I started looking up people to email to tell my story.

The first person I email was Governor. Jeb Bush I typed my whole story out and I told him something had to be done because law enforcement don't do anything unless a woman is brutally beaten or murdered oh I really went off in this letter.

I emailed the white house and told them the same thing and how my voice will be heard I told them I was contacting the media and one day I would be on the White House steps. All I kept thinking was what do I have to loose maybe someone will answer me I even emailed Oprah and Montel and Maury.

Like I said I was a woman on a mission.

After I was done emailing people, I started looking up the laws on domestic violence and printed them off. I also contacted tv.20 and Starr banner.

When I got back to the shelter it was about seven thirty P.M I made myself something to eat and watched a little television. But my mind was still on everything I did earlier that day.

I went back to my room and started reading about the laws in Florida and other states. And then I said to my self "Now I know why I am still here I am going to be the voice for other women in domestic violence situations. When I told the counselor's at the shelter what I was going to do they laughed at me and thought I was crazy.

They would just yes me to death. I asked if I could have a clipboard because I was going to start a petition. They gave it to me.

I had made some phone calls the next day one call was to the Battered Women's Project. I told them my story and asked what laws they had I told them my life was like the Tracy Thurman story "A Cry for Help". They knew exactly who I was talking about.

They were so helpful and gave me any information I wanted. I wanted to know about the anti stalking law, marital rape, if there was a law for mental abuse.

The woman on the phone said "I will find out and call you back" I didn't expect her to really call me back but the next day at nine in the morning there was a message for me to call the Battered Women Project. I was so excited I ran to the back and called her on the phone.

All I kept thinking was oh my god some one listened to me. This woman on the other end of the phone said honey "most women when they are in the shelter they are angry and want to do something but most women don't go thru with it because it is a lot of work but I hear something in your voice and I know one day I will read about you. You have a story to tell" I just laughed and couldn't thank her enough.

She had really made my day but I knew she did realize that. She did ask me to keep in touch with her and keep her updated.

I also received other numbers to other organizations like the coalition against domestic violence. They were very helpful and most of all very supportive. I told them I want to enforce the laws in Florida.

The first was anti-stalking,
The second was marital rape,
The third was coercing control, (mental abuse)

You see mental abuse is worse than physical abuse. My black and blues will go away but my nightmares will all be there. Being told you are not going to amount to anything, your are worthless, or a piece of dirt and garbage. All that stuff stay's in your mind after all you hear it enough, you believe it and no matter what anyone else says the bad stuff is easier to believe because that is all you know.

Your mind is already programmed form all the bad stuff. You can't just turn that off, it's a process you must go thru with the right counseling and right group sessions. And most of all positive support from people you can change your negative thoughts about yourself to positive, and most of all gain your self-worth back.

I remember my counselor gave me some homework that week. She gave me a journal and a goal sheet. At first I thought, what am I going to do with a journal. I had no goals, what does she expect me to do with this? she can't be serious? Oh but she was and I had to meet with her every Tuesday like clock work. I started writing in my journal and I could not stop. I loved it, I guess it was good therapy for me. I got my feeling out and felt better. I even set some goals for myself. I accomplished what I set out that week. I was surprised but I did it and felt great.

CHAPTER 8

W ELL A MONTH went by and I was writing in my journal when I had a phone message to call a very good friend of mine, and how it was very important for me to call a soon as possible.

I had got nervous, I thought oh my god what now?

I called my friends and they were very excited and said I had an email from Governor Jeb Bush. I thought I was going to die, I couldn't wait to see it but I had no computer access so I demanded they read it to me. All I kept thinking was could this be real? Did someone finally listen to me?

The email read:

"Dear Ms. Renna;

Governor Bush received your email and asked to respond.

Each state attorney is an elected official charged with certain discretionary duties, including the duty to determine whether to prosecute any particular crime committed within his or her jurisdiction.

The decision is based on the quality and quantity of the evidence of guilt shown, and in the best interest of justice. For further assistance, I encourage you to continue working with your locally elected state attorney and local law enforcement to ensure your safety. I am forwarding a copy of your letter to the Florida Department of Children and Families and the Florida Department of Law enforcement for their review. I encourage you to work with these agencies and your local officials to resolve your concerns.

As a concern citizen, you have the opportunity to influence legislation by contacting your local legislative delegation. You may wish to write to your Senator or representative. If such a bill ever comes before the Governor for signature, he will remember your views.

Thank you again for writing.

Warren Davis
Aid to the Governor
Office of Citizens Services

I was so excited I just couldn't believe they answered my email but now there was another email, this one was from Senator Bill Nelson him self.
This one said:

"Dear Ms Renna

Thank you for sharing your personal experience with domestic violence. I am very troubled by the growing domestic violence problems faced by American families.

The National Women's Health information center estimates that domestic violence is the leading cause of injury for American women between the ages of 15 and 54. Women are five to eight times more likely than men to be victims. Undoubtedly, domestic violence has a profound effect on all family members and can create a cycle of violence that lasts generations.
The Violence Against Women Act, enacted by Congressmen in 1994 And the victims of Crime Act, provides funding for programs relating to domestic violence.
Grants are approved for battered women shelters, community programs on domestic violence and counseling programs for families.

I share your concern that federal and state government work effectively together to curb the escalating numbers of domestic violence cases, and that adequate federal funding is provided I appreciate your conveying your views to me. I will keep your thoughts in mind when the Senate considers legislation regarding this issue.

Thank you,
Senator Bill Nelson

Now can you see why I was so excited, yes I sent emails out but I really didn't think I would get a response?

Was this really happening? Yes it was and now I knew what I had to do if they read my email then so will every one else maybe just maybe I can convince the media to do my story.

When I told them at the shelter what I was going to do they just looked at me like I was crazy.

Now I didn't care what anyone thought. I had to get legislators to help me, but how I don't even know who these people are I never paid any attention when they were on the news.

I started looking in the phone book but now I had to find out what district I was in.

This was all written in another language to me what and where do I start.

First I called TV20 and spoke to reporter and asked him if they covered stories on domestic violence he replied "we do some cases' and I started to tell him. He said he would be in touch with me. I waited but nothing so I said oh well its okay.

I left the shelter and went out on my own, the shelter gives you the tools and you must do the foot work and I did.

I started to make phone calls to legislator offices; the first one I contacted was State Rep Larry Cruetel. To my surprise his right hand person set a meeting up.

I was so scared after all you see these men on the news. My pastor at the time came with me.

I didn't sleep that whole night before I thought what I will say? How do I tell this man what happened to me?

I prayed for God to give me the right words and not sound like a fool. See I was told not to tell my him my story, I didn't want to sound like a victim, I was disappointed, then why was I going if I couldn't tell my story. The whole purpose was for me to get my story out.

Anyway I arrived at State Rep office at nine A.M. I sat in the waiting area This gentleman walked out of his office with a smile on his face, very soothing look.

I couldn't speak, I didn't know what to say, my body was trembling. Cruetel knew it his right hand person Gina was just looking at me. He asked me how can I help you. I couldn't speak words just wouldn't come out of my mouth.

With my hands trembling I said in a whispering voice something has to be done, and my voice started to crack. I didn't want to lose it, I didn't want to lose it, but I said again something has to be done about the laws in Florida. And I started to tell him what I went thru.

He folded his hands on his desk and said "I have wanted to do something about abuse." I said the laws in Florida needed to be enforced.

He started telling me about how passing a bill works and then said to me how would you feel about telling your story up in front of legislators in Tallahassee if they agree to hear the bill.

Once he said that about me telling my story, he couldn't shut me, up I felt comfortable and said oh I got this now. I thought to myself another person listened to me.

Harry always told me after he would make me feel like crap "Honey don't you know how special you are:"

At this point all I kept saying is yes I do know now

I had people attention. They were listening but not only were they listening they were helping and agreeing that laws In Florida needed to be enforced.

When I was leaving his office, he suggested I contact the star banner and news stations he gave me the approval to say State Rep Mr. Cruetel is working with me to amend these laws in Florida. He only had to tell me that once I was on the phone with TV20 asked for David, they said he was out in the field he'd call me back. I thought sure.

I contacted the star banner but they said the would wait till we went to Tallahassee if our bill was going to be heard. I felt they gave me the brush off. It didn't bother me though because I had others I was contacting.

That day after leaving State Rep office I went and checked my email. Once again there was an email from this author I had found on the internet His name Victor Rivers.

Victor's email read:

"Hi Dawn

Thanks for sharing your story with me; the first part in the healing process is breaking the silence. My advice would be to contact the NATIONAL NETWORK TO END DOMESTIC VIOLENCE; there's a link on my website and look up the Florida DV Coalition Link. I would write to them and tell them you have corresponded with me. ask them how you get involved or share your ideas with them. I'm not sure if your local shelter has access to my memoir's PRIVATE FAMILY MATTER, but is has a resource section in the back. Lots of people have written to say the book has helped them in the healing process and family therapists are using it in their practice.

Take care,
Peace
Victor Rivers.

Wow! My day was just getting better and better. I was basically jumping for joy. I couldn't even sleep that night all I kept thinking was ok what do I do next?

The next morning my phone rang at ten A.M. It was David Hamilton from TV20 news, ask if I was available to me taped and get my story out. I flew off the couch and yelled YES lets do this. He said he'd be there by one o'clock I said I will be ready.

Well he got tied up and was there by two in the afternoon, but it didn't bother me. Well I told him my story everything in detail. I showed him the material I had researched, I was now labeled a woman on a mission. And yes that is what I was.

After my taping with David Hamilton was over he said my story would air at 6 PM. That night I couldn't wait to see it.

He also video taped all the paper work I had put together from my research on domestic violence.

I was living in a two bedroom two bath trailer in Ocala. I had given David permission to video the outside of my trailer. I kind of forgot about my trailer number being on the trailer or maybe it was that I didn't forget I just wasn't scared of Harry anymore or his in-laws.

My voice was being heard and he knew it. Everyone would hear my story and know the type of man he really was. It turned out my story hit at 6 PM and at 11 PM the next day. On the afternoon news to my surprise the response I was getting to my story and situation was amazing. People were very supportive of me on my journey.

One day while I was at work my son Mike was home. This woman knocked on my door. This was like three months after my story aired. She left her number, I called her back.

It turned out she to was a survivor of domestic violence. She just wanted to talk to me and tell me her story. And she thanked me for being courageous and telling my story. I felt really good.

That night after she left, I seen car lights outside my home. I went out to see who it was, the truck was a small two door truck with two men in it. I could not see their faces for they turned their head. But the one in the passenger seat was writing down my license plate number. He turned his head quickly so I couldn't see it but I saw his shirt that had they symbol Cemex on hit that was the company Harry worked for.

After that, I called police and made report they watched my house closely. It was not long after that that I had moved again.

A couple of months went by and I was on my way to a lobbying session at a college to share my story. When I stopped in a convenience store.

My head was down. I was getting money out of my purse and fixing my poster on the front seat when I looked up and reached for the handle to get out of my car. There stood Harry in his work, close and he looked at me and said baby did you hear I almost died. My response to him was, I will pray for you and I walked away. The look I gave him was very cold and I guess it also showed him there was no more fear of this man there. I was ready for anything. I never turned my back on him while I walked away. Though he just stood there in amazement and got in his truck and took off.

Harry no longer had the control or hold over me and he didn't know what to expect. I guess just from the look in his eyes.

You see abusers do not like losing control that they have over a victim. See the reason they abuse is because they have very low self-esteem, no confidence about themselves so what they do is belittle their victim and destroy their self worth, their confidence to where the victim believes every word the abuser is telling them. I believe it makes the abuser feel very powerful.

That was the last time I ever saw him. I felt really good that night because I always wondered what would happen if I saw him, would I run, scream I just didn't know. But I took my power and control back that night, it felt great.

Wow! Now my voice was being heard and everyone was listening. God was making all this possible because now he had planted a seed in my heart and that was to help other women and children in my situation.

Domestic violence is a vicious cycle that goes on from one generation to the next, and that is what must come to an end.

Its funny when I would see my dad hit my mother, I use to tell her how can you put up with that, I will never let a man do to me what he does to you to me. Not in a million years.

Well I picked the same kind of men my mother did, just like my daddy.

The shelter had camera's around the building and one night at 4:30 AM I could not sleep so I went to sit with the counselor at the front desk and I glanced over to the TV screen that monitor the outside of building and there it was a green Vitar. And I let out a yell. It was Harry truck we called the police. When the cop came out he said there was nothing he could do, it was not parked on the property. It was down at the end of driveway. He was more interested in the music the councilor had on the radio than he was with Harry's car being parked near the shelter.

CHAPTER 9

I REMEMBER THE day I went to court for my restraining order against him, my advocate for women was there, my attorney. I remember asking the bailiff was Harry out there, he said yes but don't worry your attorney is there he can't hurt you.

My whole body was trembling because I knew he was going to make up lies, and I really thought he would have convinced the judge I remember the judge asking Harry questions and Harry told the judge that I was crazy. I cut my arms with knives and scissors.

How dumb was that if I did cut my arms I would have scars there is nothing on my arms or wrist except a very light mark that is a self defense position, you can tell that by looking at it.

Then the judge listen to my attorney and the judge asked me do you want anything to do with him, I answered no. My attorney asked Harry did he recall an incident were my client was woken by you penetrating her and she said no and you continued, he replied no. Then the attorney asked him again and this time he replied yes, but not on the date she said.

I thought the judge would have done something then because he had just admitted what he had done. But no surprise, nothing was done this man got away with rape, got away with stalking and a whole lot more. He tried to play the victim in the courtroom.

First of all, if you see the size of this man 6'4 I am 4'9. No one bought the fact he was a victim here. Picture it, I come up to his belly.

Anyway, I was granted my restraining order for one year. It bothered me because how can they only give it to me for a year, but you know what a restraining order is, only a piece of paper.

The night I went to meet some friends at Dunkin' Donuts and we were stating outside and my back was facing the road. My friend said to me, get inside I asked why, I wasn't thinking.

As I was going into the store I turned and spotted Harry's green Vitar, I then ran in. My friends stood outside to see which way it went, I said he must be on his way to work. Maybe he didn't see me, I am safe.

He made a u turn and came back down the road. We left and started to go to Subway Restaurant. We were walking hear he made another turn and was right along side of us never said a word. I grabbed my cell phone and dialed 911. I said where I was and what was happening. As the cops were coming down the road, Harry took off.

The cop said they have to catch him following me because I told them he is stalking me.

Well stalking is very hard to prove.

But with everything that had happened to me, I am the strongest woman now than I ever was.

I thought about how my story will help others in my situation it may even save someone's life. I had decided to start my own non profit organization for women and children or actually any one of abuse.

I decided to name it "Dawn Renna's Women In Healing Inc." So now I started researching non profit organizations. How they work and the INS and out of them the domestic violence shelter was not very supportive of what I wanted to do.

They said a lot of women walk through the doors angry and say they are going to do this and they are going to do that. I don't think they realize I am not most women, I am a survivor. I have a been like that since I was a child, I had to.

I only had me to turn to I would hit rock bottom and have to pull myself up no one else was going to do it.

As I sit and write and hope my story will help you, I listen to my worship music, and smile, I could have chose to stay a victim and drown in self pity. And maybe would have stay in the situation I was instead of looking for help.

Yes it took many years before I looked to organization or someone to help me. But I choose victory instead of being a victim.

As you may already know, I live by faith and put all my trust into the Lord. He is my salvation. Without God in my life, I am nothing. After all he gave his only Son to die on across for our sins and that is the reason all my sins were washed away. He forgave me of my sins.

My biggest optical was me forgiving me and learning to let go.

Before I could have done all this I had to forgive my abuser for what he did in order for me to move on before I could forgive me.

I am still learning to let go of things. You know the saying, let go, let God.

CHAPTER 10

ON FEBRUARY 14, 2007 I went on to and filed my papers for my domain name, 'DAWN Renna'S WOMEN IN HEALING INC'. I took the first step to my dream. After that I filed for my EIN, number which is an employee identification number. It is something you need so people can identify your business, after that you must file for your 501c3 form for non-profit organizations.

When I had started my research on Domestic Violence Laws these were the ones that had started me on my journey:

In 1979 after twelve black women were murdered in Boston a public out cry about the lack of media attention to violence against women of color lead to the formation of the Conbahee River coalition.

In 1985 Thurman vs. Torrington is the first federal case in which a battered women sued a city for police failure to protect her from her husband's violence.

Tracy Thurman who remains scarred and partially paralyzed from stab wounds inflicted by her husband wins two million judgment against the city suits lead to Connecticut passage of mandatory arrest laws.

Tracy Thurman is the woman I would tell everyone if they have seen her story "A Cry For Help", that was what I was living the same exact thing except I was lucky to get out.

Back in 1993 in this introduction to the U.S Senate Judicial Committee report violence against women.

The response to rape detours on the road to equal justice Senator Joseph Biden stated the findings reveal a justice system that fails by any standard to meet its goals apprehending conviction and incarcerating violent criminals. 98% of the victims of rape never see there attackers caught tried or imprisoned.

When I read that on the computer at the library, I just felt that is so true.

Well then back in 1994 President Clinton signs the violence against women act as part of the violent crime control and law enforcement act of 1994 the act provided 156 million dollars in state grants to bolster legal law enforcement prosecution and victim services to better address violence against women.

And then there was 1997 were President Clinton signed anti stalking lawn which makes interstate stalking and harassment a federal offense even if the victim has not obtained a protection order.

WOMEN IN HEALING INC. is a transitional housing were women and children or actually anyone of abuse can reside for six months to a year so that they can learn the coping skills they need to live productive lives without feeling they must go back to their abuser.

It is not a shelter. It is transitional housing. They will come to women in healing after they have completed the program at a domestic violence shelter.

The DV shelter supplies you with the tools you need, but of course you have to do the rest.

After I applied for the paper work, I received a letter of congratulations and let me just say the day I received that was the happiest day of my life.

See all my life, I was told you are not going to amount to nothing. All I could think of was Ha look at me now.

But I wasn't doing this all for me. I am doing this for all victims of any kind of abuse. It don't necessarily mean only for women and children it is also for men.

There are men being abused physically and mentally but they are usually to proud to come forth because they are worried what will people think. After all, I am a man. I just want to say no one is immuned. Anyone can be a victim.

I had done a lobbing session up at CFCC community college and to my surprise men were coming up to me, signing my petition and asking question. It was funny someone was there representing me from State Rep Larry Cruetel office and she pointed out that there was a gentlemen sitting on the other side of us easing his way closer and closer. So I decided to take my petition over to him and speak with him and he started asking, well what if you are a man and an ex girlfriend is following you all over calling you twenty four hours a day sending you letters and just wont leave you alone. She show's up anywhere and every where and I said that is considered stalking and gave him a number to call.

He said he had a problem because his friends and family would make fun of him and I told him my story.

He signed my petition, thanked me and said I helped him. I wasn't sure how I did that but I felt good about it afterwards.

All my life I loved helping people, I could help someone else so easy but when it came to me I had no clue.

I went to a seminar at the Hilton. It was on Human Trafficking. I used to hear, watch movies on television about it but was not aware that it was really happening. That seminar opened my eyes and let me tell you, I was left with my mouth open.

I was so happy I went it should me that there are all types of abuse some more server than others but abuse is abuse no matter what category. All communities need to come together in all aspect of this situation.

I even look at homeless people a lot different these days because when they would come up to me and ask me for change, I use to say you know there are jobs out there I never thought about what their story may be. It never even crossed my mind.

But after being there, if I have a dollar or something I will give it to them to get something to eat.

I am saying this to you, for you just to remember everyone has a story we just don't know it.

Someone asked me what you would say to other women in your situation. I would just let them know there is hope out there, don't give up. Don't let someone tell you that you're worthless. It is just a way to control you. You are worth something. You are a human being, go into the phone book, there are numbers all in there were you can call organization for help.

I know it sounds easy for me to say but I also know it's not that easy to leave.

This is what I hope the women get out of 'Women in Healing', self worth, independence and most of all self esteem.

You have to believe in your self for others to believe in you. That was what I learned. I also had to learn to love me because if I didn't love me, no one else would either.

I am hoping what I learned other women and victims of any situation will learn the same thing. Its like a baby learning to walk, you have to learn how to live after abuse. Its like taking your first step, but it's the step of being free. The feeling of freedom is awesome.

There are a lot of places that are in desperate need of transitional housing. I have talked to people in other states that think what I am doing is great and especially because of were I came from and were I am now.

You know people talk about college degrees but I look at it like this, my abuser didn't need a college degree to beat me or I didn't need a college degree to receive the beaten. No one gave me a certificate for being abused.

Education is very important, and I would love to earn my college degree and one day I will have it. I now know that I can do anything I set my mind to. So can anyone else in this world.

I really hope my book can inspire others to never give up. And it's okay to fight for what you believe in; just because one person won't listen does not mean others won't either.

Put your faith and trust in God above. When you do that you can move mountains.

Harry had bought me a Bible. The name of it was the "THE NOBIES WHO BECAME SOMEBODIE". I thought to myself sure, now he is trying to say that I am a nobody, but after reading it, I know its all in the power of prayer.

I am excited about WOMEN IN HEALING because I see were it is going. I have a long road ahead of me but I know in the end it will all be worth it.

I quit my job to work on the organization it was time to devote every minute of the day to what I really wanted.

I had jobs in Denny's Cracker-Barrel but my heart wasn't there. I wanted to be working in the field that I know so well and where my story may save someone's life.

Because their thoughts might be, "Wow! if she can do it so can I."

When I got fired from Cracker-Barrel all I kept thinking is why am I being fired? I did nothing wrong, I didn't understand.

How could they have said I was a no call no show when I was not even on the schedule. And then I walked into my friends church were she goes and the bishop and pastor came to me took the oil and said, "You lost your job but watch what God is about to do."

I was amazed how did they know this? I thought it was God.

The next day my land lord core knocked on my door. He was standing in my kitchen and then he left but it was like he wanted to ask me something, but a few minutes after he left he came back and said how my story touched him so much he wanted to do something for others.

I invited him in and started telling him about the organization I have started and now he is president on my advisory board.

Look at God. That is what I mean let go and let God. Put all your faith and trust in the Lord.

I know you may be going through tough times and some people want living proof. Well, I am a living proof and I am a walking testimony.

God spared my life when I knew I should have been dead. I am just sorry it took me so long to find Jesus.

See Women In Healing is something God said has to happen. This is what He wants and He now made it possible

It took me a whole year to get my story in star banner but they ran it and told my whole story.

It's all in God's time, not mine.

As I sit and write this book somewhere out there, a woman is being beaten or even murdered. We must come together as one and show the abusers that we are in control now and we take out power and control back.

Many people think I am crazy for trying to do what I am doing but I learned I don't care what people think of me. I only care what God thinks of me and how I live my life. Because I walk with the Lord, I don't fear anyone or anything,

You see there is no fear in the kingdom of heaven.

My mission statement for Women In Healing is:

"Transitional housing for women and children of domestic violence to learn a new way of life without abuse and to walk in the sprit of the Lord."

CHAPTER 11

FOR THE FIRST time since I could remember, me and my children have the best relationship now. See for a long time, my older son wasn't talking to me because I was with my abuser. We didn't talk for over a year so he had no clue as to what was going on with me. He heard rumors that I was still getting high, and of course believed everything he heard.

I didn't blame him when he told me, but anyway one day when I went to wall-mart to see if I could get them to sponsor Women In Healing Inc. I spotted his girlfriend walking in the store with their baby. I wasn't sure if I should say anything after all she hates me. But I wanted to see my granddaughter even if it was just for a few seconds. I had never seen her before.

I remember just standing there and asking God what should I do. What is the worst that can happen? The most she could do is walk away or not answer me right?

Well I waited for her to walk toward me and I said hello. To my surprise she answered me, all I wanted to do was hold my granddaughter at that time but I never asked her. My whole body was shaking, I just wanted to grab the baby hug and kiss her. My first grandbaby and she was now 5 months old. I have a little extra money on me so I asked if I could buy the baby something's. She okayed it and we shopped for a little while she said she would go and talk to my son.

I told her that when I was in the hospital with chest pain and they had to do a cardiac cath. I had called my sister and asked her to please call my son and tell him I wanted to make amends with him. But at that time, he didn't want to but his girlfriend said she would call me after she talked to him.

She had told me that his ex was making up lies about me said I was all strung out on drugs. Meanwhile, I was not even in the area. I was working out of town, they also told him that I was still with my abuser. But anyway, she went home with the bags of stuff I bought the baby. My son said to her were did you get all that stuff for the baby? She told him from her grandma. He thought it was her mom but she said no your mother. She also said he started shaken and wanted my number. That evening, I picked Mike up and went over to their house. All I did was hold my oldest son tight and cried and he cried. We are closer now than we ever was. I just praise God once again for bringing my family back.

All my sons are happy and they all see each other again. And my granddaughter Marianna is just so beautiful and precious. I am blessed to be part of her life. I am grateful when I heard her say grandma for the first time. I cried, I never thought I would be called grandma. It is like music to my ears. I love that little girl with all my heart and soul and because of what my son AJ seen me go through, he is just the best dad I have ever seen. I am so proud of him. I hope he realizes that.

I haven't celebrated holidays in a really long time but now I am going all out. I have beautiful home and my family is back, praise God. Not to mention my life and really good friends that I can trust with everything I got and I know they would never hurt me.

I know my mother is watching me from heaven. and I know she is very proud of me.

She used to kid me when I was a child because I was always writing poems and she said to me "you could write a book" and then we'd laugh.

Here are 2 of the poems I wrote when I was still 19 years old and was experiencing depression:

Depression

Depression is a lonely feeling
that leaves you all alone and dealing with the pain
you feel inside
that can't even be described and makes you
always feel deprived.

Everyone tells you that they care
and that they will always be there
so you try and talk to them and make them understand
but they don't listen all they do is demand.

so you ran to hide and all you did was cried
after that you found that all you did was lied.

depression makes you insecure
i always thought I knew for sure that my life was very
pure and I never needed any cure.
but now I am not so sure
how much more pain must I endure
before there really is a cure

depression makes you hurt so bad and makes you
feel your going mad I am so tired of always being sad
I always felt inside me a hurting pain but always
found someone to blame now the day finally came
and I realize its no longer a game
for all I do is cry in vain.

please help me find a cure I am so unsure all I want
is to be pure. I am tired of feeling all this pain
its making me feel insane I am tired of crying out in
in vain

there's days I sit and watch the birds fly by
and wonder why can't I
I know that must sound absurd but I really wish I was
bird. Lord why can't it be all I want is to be free.
Lord I hope you hear my plea and put and end to all
my pain and misery
please come for me and set me free
oh how beautiful it would be to live without
all this pain and misery.

Life

Life is a part of nature
a place of gods creature
Life is a precious thing
and there is so much happiness it can bring

Life is something we must treasure
nothing else could ever measure
Life is what we make it even though we try and fake it

Love is a special thing that two people share
but it really hurts when you find your partner
really don't care
that is when life seems so unfair

love is a part of life
even though it feels like you have been cut by a knife
but that is no reason to give up on life

enjoy your life until the end
remember a broken heart will always mend

their is only one person on whom you can always
depend on until the end

and that my friend is
God above to stand by you
and give you love . . .

Now look at me, my story will help someone realize that hey I don't have to take this anymore I too can survive.

I can choose victory not victim but it will be up to you to decide. Some people say well if there is really a God then why did this happen to me. God can control all of thing but he cannot control a person will . . .

Amen.

I am know enrolled in training for the guardian ad litem program which is were you go into the court and be the voice for a child who is either abused, neglected etc.

It feels so good to be doing for others. It is a very rewarding feeling, you couldn't even begin to imagine.

I feel honored because God is giving me a chance or shall I say God has in trusted me with His desire for what it is He wants to be done for victims.

I know He will guide me with the wisdom for the women and children of abuse. This is His will, not my will. And what means more than anything is my family is a part of all this.

AJ said to me one day when I showed him my story on the news with TV20, Wow, mom I am looking forward to when the baby grows up to bring her past your building for Women In Healing and telling her look that is grandma's building and tell her all about it.

He was so proud I could see it in his eyes. That meant more to me than anything in this world. I finally gave my kids a reason to be proud of me.

CHAPTER 12

OCTOBER IS DOMESTIC Violence Awareness Month. I never knew that but it is were survivor tell their story, and the one's that didn't survivor are remembered. It is also were the public can attend workshops to learn more about domestic violence. You don't have to be a victim to attend, you just have to want to learn more about the help that is out there.

You may not be a victim but you may know someone that is. Don't get frustrated when you tell them to leave their abuser and they don't, its not that easy to just get up and leave. There is a lot of reasons victims stay it could be, because they are petrified to leave fear of their abuser finding them.

It could be financial reason "oh how will I support myself and my children" I don't want my kids to grow up with out a dad or mom if you're a man Most of all it's because they think "I have nowhere to go" or What will my family think?

Just be patient if you can I know it is frustrating because you have helped so many times before but they keep going back. Don't give up just let the person know that you will be there when they are ready.

My advice to anyone who is a victim and is still in the relationship is pack an emergency bag. Keep it where you can get to it quick where your abuser can't find it. Put important papers in there that you will need. Plan an escape path if you can. Use the phone for 911 or ask a neighbor if they hear anything to call 911 immediately.

There is even a save a friend hotline number. My suggestion to you is get out while there is still time before its too late.

In the state attorney's office there is a poem hanging on the wall and here it is. I am putting it in here just in case you never seen it. It's written by an unknown author:

"I Got Flowers Today"

I got flowers today. It wasn't my
Birthday or any other special day.
We had our first argument last night
And he said a lot of cruel things that really hurt me
I know he is sorry and didn't mean the things he said.

Because he sent me flowers today

I got flowers today. It wasn't our anniversary or any other special day.
Last night he threw me into a wall and started to choke me
It seemed like a nightmare
I couldn't believe it was real,
I woke up this morning sore and bruised all over
I know he must be sorry,

Because he sent me flowers today

I got flowers today and it wasn't Mothers day or any other special day,
Last night he beat me up again.
And it was much worse than all the other times
If I leave him what will I do?
How will I take care of my kids?
What about money?
I am afraid of him and I am scared to leave
But I know he must be sorry

Because he sent me flowers today

I got flowers today. Today was a very special day
It was the day of my funeral
Last night he finally killed me
He beat me to death.
If only I gathered
Enough courage and strength to leave him

I would not have gotten flowers today

Unknown Author

The first time I read that poem was in the state attorney's office when he told me there wasn't enough evidence. all I could say was oh my God, I took a couple of copies of the poem that day. I believed it kept me from going back to my abuser because I knew the next step for me was death except I knew he would not have gotten his hands dirty, he would have gotten one of his crack attic friends to do it. But I knew he would have gone thru with all the threats he made.

I stapled the poem to all the posters I made when I went to lobby at the colleges. I also put it in with my booklet that I made for the cover of my petition that I gave to State Rep office.

I remember the look on their face when they read it. I guess no one read it in a long time because I know it has been around for a while. I remember living in New York and seeing it in the court house there. I never thought it could be me one day.

I learned never say never.

I am also putting in hear another thing I have on my poster I received this when I was in the shelter it is important to me because it also opened my eyes.

The reason I am putting these in my book is because if you're not sure your ready to leave yet these are some of the tools you can read to show that the shelter can help. The program varies from one to another but when you go in, you have to work the program otherwise you're wasting your time and theirs they give you tools and you must do the foot work.

There tools can really help you if you apply yourself. This one that works for me is called

A CREED TO LIVE BY

Do not undermine your worth
By comparing yourself to others.
It is because we are different
That each of us is special

Do not set your goals
By what other people deem important
Only you know
What is best for you?

Do not take for granted
The things closest to your heart.
Cling to them as you would your life.
For with out them
Life is meaningless.

Do not let your life
Slip through your fingers
By living in the past
Nor for the future
By living your life one day at a time
You live all the days of your life

Do not give up
When you still have something to give
Nothing is really over
Until the moment you stop trying
It is a fragile thread
That binds us to each other

Do not be afraid to encounter risks
It's by taking chances
That we learn how to be brave

Do not shut love out of your life
By saying it is impossible to find.

The quickest way to receive love
Is to give love
The fastest way to loose love
Is to hold it too tightly
In addition
The best way to keep love
Is to give it wings.

Do not dismiss your dreams
To be without dreams
Is to be without hope
To be without hope
Is to be without purpose
Do not through life
So fast that you forget
Not only were you have been
But also were you are going
Life is not a race
But a journey to be savored.

I remember the day I received this in the shelter it was during my group session. I loved it from the first time we had to read it, I have tried to live by it since I got it.

When I was in the shelter like I said, they gave me tools I did applied them. I made all my group even parenting skills.

The most important thing I learned was in my group sessions, I always thought I was alone and no one could identify with me but I was dead wrong.

It helped me to speak with others who came from the same place I did.

There is also after care and you don't have to reside there to get help or go to groups you can go even without residing there. You will still have a counselor and go to rape crises groups.

When you are a victim of domestic violence every one in your family becomes a victim especially your children. Because of what your abuser did to you and dominated you, sometimes the victims turn it around and take it out on the kids. It don't necessarily have to be hitting it just can be screaming because she you were dominated so now you may look to dominate someone and 98% of the time it is the kids that the victim takes it out on with out even realize you are doing it.

I never hit my kids but I became a screamer and I would yell a lot. I don't do it anymore when someone pointed it out to me. I said oh my God, how could I do that. It wasn't them or their fault.

I caught myself, when I realized what I was doing. I changed it I didn't want to be known as oh my mother scream's at me really bad I am scared.

Now I try to shelter my kids from any stupid nonsense. I wish I knew then what I know now.

I wasn't required to take the parenting skills class when I was at the shelter because I refused to have my kids in shelter with me. But I took the class anyway, I learned a lot from it. I wish I could have gone for help a long time ago. I just wasn't aware of the services out there and I was afraid. But you know what the Bible says there is no fear in the kingdom of heaven. The only thing I fear is disappointing the Lord above. He is the only one I have to answer to but his love is all I need.

I have more now than ever before and that is because I choose to live each day for my God who gave His only son to die on the cross for my sins. I really hope my story helps you or someone you know.

Even if you are not a victim of domestic violence and your reading this I hope it gives you the opportunity to seek the Lord and praise him every day just for waking you up.

Please help us stop the violence. We all must come together so wherever you live, look into doing something in your community. Don't wait until a women or child or any one is murder because of domestic violence before you do something to help. Go online and see what you can do to help stop the violence.

Remember you don't have to be a victim, you too can have victory. Sometimes we don't even know we are victims.

Here are some questions for you:

1) Does your partner call you stupid?
2) Does he or she make fun of you in front of your friends or family?
3) Does he or she make you feel like you can't do anything right?
4) Does your partner make statements like your nothing with me?
5) Does he or she control your ever move?
6) Do you feel scared sometime of how your partner will act if you say or do something?
7) Has he threatended to kill you?
8) Are you afraid he is going to kill you ?
9) What are you most afraid of ?
10) Has he threatened you with a gun or a knife?
11) Has he ever choked you ?
12) Has he ever abused animals infront of you?
13) Has he threatened to kill himself ?
14) Is he keeping track of your movements ?
15) Have you recently seperated ?

If you answered yes to any of these questions I suggest you call your your local DV shelter and speak with a counselor.

I remember when I looked at these questions and there were a lot more questions too, but I answered yes to most of them they are warning signs that you are in a abusive relationship.

I also learned that my abuser broke down my self esteem for the simple fact he had no self esteem so it made him feel good to kill myself, confidence and self worth. That is what they do to make them feel in control.

You are worth much more than that and you can take control back. You may not be going through any of this stuff I spoke about in my book, but you may no someone else who is you can help there is a save a friend hotline number.

Don't get frustrated if someone you know is not ready to leave it just may be they are too scared of their partner especially if there are kids involved, just don't turn you back on them,

Let them know you will be there to support them in any decision they make because trust me, there will come that day were something will click and they say enough is enough, I want my life back.

Too many people get frustrated and just walk away from friend or family member that is in abusive relationship because they feel I helped all I can and you won't leave.

Like I said earlier, it's not that easy just leave and you don't know how that feel's unless you're in that situation.

I really hope my story helped you or someone you know get an understanding of why we victim stay.

I hope this also gives someone the courage to leave and get out of the relationship and seek help from organizations that are out there your life may depend on it. I am in the processes now of putting my web site up it will be www.Dawn Renna's Women In Healing.org

There will be a comment section. I would love to know if my story helped you or someone you know in anyway.

I pray I gave you the courage to seek help.

Remember the saying always

"God, grant me the serenity
To accept the things I cannot change
The courage to change
The things I can
And the wisdom to know the difference"

The first time I ever heard that I fell to my knees and thank God for making me aware of it.

I heard it in my very first N.A. meeting and held it close to me through my ordeal; it is what I call my creed to live by.

I want to thank everyone that inspired me to write my story especially my family I got a lot out of writing this.

I give god the praise for bringing people into my life that stood by me and helped me while I went through my ordeal. I just want to give back what was given to me.

God bless all of you and keep the faith. Never let go of your dreams. Don't let someone tell you, you can't do something. You can do or be anything you set your mind to.

Look at me I am a walking testimony.

By
"Dawn Renna"